Grandpa
Tell Me Your Memories

Created by Kathleen Lashier

Copyright © 2012 Linkages

To contact the author:

Linkages

Linkages Memory Journals • P.O. Box 8282 • Des Moines, IA 50301
888-815-9063
www.mymemoryjournals.com

Printed in the U.S.A.
by G&R Publishing Co.

ISBN-13: 978-1-56383-414-1
ISBN-10: 1-56383-414-6

Distributed by:

CQProducts

507 Industrial Street • Waverly, IA 50677
800-887-4445 • Fax 800-886-7496

What was your day
and date of birth?

Where were you born?
Be specific.

Do you know any other circumstances of your birth (who was present, who delivered, etc.)?

January 3

If you have a childhood picture for me, put it in this space.

January 4

Name your brothers and sisters and their years of birth.

January 5

*What was your
mother's full name?*

January 6

*What were your
mother's date/place and
circumstances of birth?*

January 7

What was your father's
full name?

What was your father's
date/place and
circumstances of birth?

Name all the street addresses you can recall and/or all the communities you've lived in and years there.

January 10

January 11

What did your father do for a living?

January 12

Did your mother work outside the home?

Tell a nickname your family gave you and how you got it.

*Tell of any other nicknames
in your family.*

January 15

*Tell a fond memory
of your Grandpa.*

January 16

Tell a fond memory
of your Grandma.

Tell about a favorite Aunt.

Tell about a favorite Uncle.

January 17

January 18

January 19

*Relate an experience
or memory of a cousin.*

January 20

*Did any relatives ever
live with you? If not, then
relate another memory of
cousins, aunts or uncles.*

January 21

In what way did your
mother usually discipline?

January 22

How did your
father discipline?

January 23

*Tell about the naughtiest
thing you ever did.*

January 24

*If you got caught,
describe the consequences.*

January 25

*Did you ever see a President
or Vice-President in person?*

*Which of the Presidents in your
lifetime has been your favorite and why?*

January 26

*Did you ever have an
imaginary friend?*

January 27

*What did you and your
brothers or sisters fight
about the most?*

January 28

*Tell about an experience or
event that drew you together.*

January 29

*Tell about the worst winter storm
that you can remember as a child.*

January 30

*What did you use to go sledding
down a hill in the snow?*

January 31

What extras did you use for your
snowman's face, buttons, arms, hat, etc?

February 1

Tell of someone
you envied, and why.

February 2

Do you remember the first movie
you ever saw and who starred in it?

February 3

What have been some of
your very favorite movies?

How did you first
smash a finger?

*Who was the most famous
person you ever met as a child?*

*Tell about someone who had
a big influence on your life.*

*Tell about another
influential person in your life.*

Tell about a big lie you told.

*Tell about your first
favorite television shows.*

Who was your first girlfriend?

Tell about the Valentine Day festivities at your school.

Tell about a special valentine you once gave.

Tell about a special valentine you once received.

Tell about your first date.

_____
_____
_____
_____
_____
_____

February 15

Tell about your first kiss.

_____
_____
_____
_____

February 16

*What was your favorite
meal as a child?*

_____
_____
_____
_____

February 17

*Tell about family reunions
in your childhood.*

February 18

*What do you remember as
your favorite subject in school?*

February 19

What do your remember
as your least favorite
school subject?

February 20

What is the biggest
problem you remember
having in Grade School?

February 21

*What is the biggest problem you
remember having in Jr. High school?*

February 22

*What is the biggest problem you
remember having in Sr. High school?*

February 23

*Tell about a great victory or personal
success story from your school days.*

February 24

*Did you and your friends ever
have a secret hide-out?*

February 25

*Tell about a favorite restaurant
or public place where you and
your friends liked to gather.*

February 26

*Tell about the best
pet you ever had.*

February 27

*Tell about other
pets you had.*

February 28

*Tell about being in a
school play or program.*

March 1

*Tell about a school
principal you remember.*

March 2

Did you ever pretend to be sick as an excuse to stay home from school?

March 3

Did you ever get in trouble for saying a bad word?

March 4

Tell about how you spent your Saturdays during the school year.

March 5

*Tell about how you
spent your Sundays.*

March 6

*What was the naughtiest or meanest
thing you remember doing in school?*

March 7

*What were the
consequences?*

March 8

Tell of a difficult essay or
term paper assignment.

March 9

What radio programs or
stations were your favorites?

March 10

Tell of a childhood illness.

Did your parents have a favorite remedy for when you were sick or hurt?

*Did kids ever tease
you and why?*

*Do you remember
your first pizza?*

If you went to college, tell which
college you chose and why.

Tell your major and
how you chose it.

March 15

March 16

Did people wear green
on St. Patrick's Day?

March 17

Do you have any other memories
of St. Patrick's Day as a youth?

March 18

Describe some household
chores you had as a child.

March 19

*Describe some
outside chores.*

March 20

*Which chore did you dislike the most
and how did you try to get out of it?*

Did you have a favorite chore?

March 21

What bones have you
broken and how?

Did you ever
need stitches?

Do you have any other good
stories about being injured?

Tell about an experience
at the doctor's office.

March 25

Tell about an experience
at the dentist's office.

March 26

What do you remember as your
favorite time of year? Why?

March 27

If you ever hitch-hiked, explain.

March 28

*Name your best
school friends.*

*Tell of a nickname given to you by
friends or classmates. How did you
get it? How did you feel about it?*

What were some crazy names
or nicknames in your school?

March 31

Do you have a good
April Fool's Day story?

April 1

Tell about a practical joke or
prank you played on someone.

April 2

Tell about a practical joke or
prank someone played on you?

Did you ever make a kite?
How? Tell about your
kite-flying experiences.

What was your best talent?
What other things were you
really good at doing?

April 5

As a child, what did you want
to be when you grew up?

April 6

Did you ever bring home or try to adopt a wild animal?

_____

_____

_____

_____

_____

_____

April 7

Relate a favorite spring memory.

_____

_____

_____

_____

_____

April 8

Did your Mom or Dad ever find something you had hidden?

_____

_____

_____

_____

_____

April 9

Make up a limerick about yourself.
There once was a…

Now make up a limerick about me.
There once was a…

Share a memory of going to
church as you were growing up. ....

....

....

....

....

....

....

....

....

April 12

Share a memory about a
church social activity. ....

....

....

....

....

....

....

....

....

April 13

*(If the following Easter topics do not apply, please share
your special Holiday memories and traditions.)*

Tell about an Easter Egg hunt.

April 14

**If your family went to Easter
Sunrise services, tell about it.**

April 15

Tell about any other
Easter traditions.

_____

_____

_____

_____

_____

_____

_____

_____

_____

_____

April 16

When you played make-believe,
what did you pretend?

_____

_____

_____

_____

_____

_____

_____

_____

_____

April 17

If you could return to your childhood,
what would you do differently?

April 18

Is there anything you would
do differently as a teenager?

April 19

Did you ever write something
that you were really proud of?

April 20

What is the best book you
ever read as a youth?

April 21

Since you've grown, what
has been your favorite book?

April 22

*Did you have
any superstitions?*

April 23

*Where were your best
hide-and-seek places?*

April 24

*Tell about the first time you were
ever behind the wheel of a car.*

April 25

*Did you ever take anything
that wasn't yours?*

April 26

*What did you do with it?
Did you get caught?*

April 27

*Do you have a story
about a big surprise?*

April 28

*What childhood fear
do you remember?*

April 29

How much do you remember
paying for an ice cream cone?

April 30

Tell about a
May Day tradition.

May 1

What were May Baskets made of
and what did they contain?

May 2

Did you have
a treehouse?

May 3

Were you ever
bitten by a dog?

May 4

Did your mother ever
make a special gift for you?

May 5

Tell a favorite memory
of your mother.

May 6

Tell about some good advice
your mother gave you.

Relate your family Mother's Day
traditions, or tell me more about
what kind of person your mother was.

*What did you learn
from your mother?*

May 9

*Name some popular hit
songs from your youth.*

May 10

*What was your favorite
singing group or band?*

_____

_____

_____

_____

_____

_____

May 11

*Tell a favorite singer and
a song that he/she sang?*

_____

_____

_____

_____

_____

May 12

*What kind of dances did
you do as a youth?*

_____

_____

_____

_____

_____

May 13

*Tell about the first
dance you ever went to.* ....

....

....

....

*Did your high school have
a prom or formal dance.* ....

....

....

....

....

May 14

*Describe your military
experience or that of
someone in your family.* ....

....

....

....

....

....

May 15

Share a memory involving a war
during your childhood or youth.

May 16

May 17

What early childhood rhymes
or songs do you remember?

If you have another photograph of
your childhood to share, place it here.

What year did you graduate from high school? What do you recall about your feelings, emotions, hopes and dreams at this time of your life?

May 20

May 21

Tell about your graduation exercises or traditions. How many students were in your graduating class?

May 22

*Did you have homework
during your school years?* ....

....

....

....

....

....

....

....

....

May 23

*What was the dumbest stunt pulled
by you and a brother or sister?* ....

....

....

....

....

....

....

....

May 24

Were there consequences?

*Tell about Memorial Day
traditions during your youth.*

*Share a special memory
of Memorial Day.*

May 27

*Did you play a
musical instrument?*

May 28

*Tell about the closest friend
you had during your childhood.*

May 29

Is there anything you have now that
you have kept from your childhood?

May 30

Do you have any good
bathtime stories?

May 31

*Did you have a favorite nature
place you liked to explore?*

June 1

*Describe a place you
liked to go to be alone.*

June 2

*Did you ever sleep
under the stars?*

June 3

*Tell about hot dog or
marshmallow roasting.*

June 4

Did you ever go on a camp out? Tell about it.

June 5

Did you ever go on a snipe hunt?

June 6

*Do you remember a favorite
snack that you liked to make?* _____

_____

_____

_____

_____

_____

_____

June 7

*Tell about one of the first
meals you ever prepared?* _____

_____

_____

_____

_____

_____

June 8

*What was your first job?
How much did you get paid?* _____

_____

_____

_____

_____

June 9

*Tell about other paying
jobs you had as a youth.*

June 10

*Tell about a strange person
that lived in your town.*

June 11

*If you were ever in
a parade, tell about it.*

June 12

*Tell another memory
about a parade.*

June 13

*Share a childhood memory
about a death that affected you.*

June 14

*Relate your happiest
memory as a youth.*

June 15

How did you learn to swim?

June 16

Where did you go swimming?

June 17

*Tell a favorite memory
of your father.*

June 18

*Tell about some good
advice your father gave you.*

June 19

Relate your family Father's Day traditions, or tell me more about what kind of person your father was.

June 20

Did your father ever make a special gift for you?

June 21

*What did you learn
from your father?*

_____

_____

_____

_____

_____

_____

_____

_____

_____

June 22

*Did you ever go
skinny-dipping?*

_____

_____

_____

Did you ever make mud pies?

_____

_____

_____

June 23

Were you ever chased
by an animal? _____

_____

_____

_____

_____

_____

_____

_____

June 24

Did you go barefoot in the summer?
If so, relate an experience about _____
stepping on something. _____

_____

_____

_____

_____

_____

_____

_____

June 25

As a youth, did you do any craft,
sewing, stitching or needlework?

June 26

Tell about a bike you had.

June 27

Tell about your
first very own car.

June 28

*Did you ever have
or make a swing?*

June 29

*Tell about seeing something you
thought was very beautiful.*

June 30

*Describe an outside
game you made up.*

July 1

Describe an inside
game you made up.

What kind of fireworks did people
have when you were a youth?

*Tell about Independence Day
traditions of your childhood.*

July 4

*Do you have a special July 4th
that you remember most?*

July 5

Did you ever go to carnivals or amusement parks? Where?

_____

_____

_____

_____

_____

July 6

What kinds of rides and games were there? How much did they cost?

_____

_____

_____

_____

July 7

Tell about any State Fair or County Fair experiences.

_____

_____

_____

_____

July 8

Tell about going to a circus, a Chautauqua, or a hometown celebration/festival.

July 9

Tell any favorite summertime memory.

July 10

*Did you go fishing, hunting
or trapping in your youth?*

July 11

*Tell about your
biggest or best catch.*

July 12

Do you remember having a favorite candy? How much did it cost?

July 13

Share a horse-riding story.

July 14

Share a memory about going on a picnic.

July 15

*What kinds of party games or
party activities were popular?*

_____

_____

_____

_____

_____

_____

_____

_____

_____

_____

July 16

*Share a memory involving
a heatwave or drought.*

_____

_____

_____

_____

_____

_____

_____

_____

_____

July 17

*What did you
do to stay cool?*

July 18

*What was your favorite
holiday of the year? Why?*

July 19

Share a birthday
party memory.

Tell about the neatest shoes
you ever owned as a youth.

*Share a memory
about a power outage.*

July 22

*Relate a memory involving
a flood or cloudburst.*

July 23

*Relate a memory of a tornado,
hurricane, or destructive wind.*

July 24

*What memories do you
have of lightning or thunder
during your childhood?*

July 25

*Share a special memory
about riding in a boat.*

July 26

*Tell about a family
vacation trip.*

July 27

*Share the best vacation
experience you can recall.*

July 28

*Share the most unpleasant
vacation experience you can recall.*

July 29

*Do you have any other
memories about a river,
lake, or beach to share?*

July 30

*Tell a memory about riding
on a ferry, bus, train, or plane.*

July 31

*Describe a proud moment
from your childhood.*

August 1

*Describe your
childhood home.*

August 2

Describe your neighborhood.

August 3

Tell about your bedroom.

August 4

*Tell a memory about having company
at your house, or of a family party.*

*Tell about board games and card
games you played as a youth.*

*Tell about card
games you played.*

Do you have any
knowledge of how your
first name was chosen?

Do you have any knowledge about
the origins of your family name?

*Tell about a time
when you got lost.*

*Did you ever play in
the sprinkler or hose?*

Share an experience about
poison ivy, poison weed,
bee stings or bug bites.

August 12

Did you have any favorite family
songs that you sang together?

August 13

*Tell of an experience climbing
a mountain or a big hill.*

August 14

*Share a memory of staying
overnight with a friend.*

August 15

*If you ever ran away
from home, tell about it.*

August 16

Do you remember being really
curious about something?

Share your childhood
experiences with roller skates.

*Did you ever experience
home sickness?*

*Tell about a favorite,
or least favorite
baby-sitter you had.*

*Share an early
experience with shaving.*

August 21

*Tell about a favorite doll,
teddy bear, or other stuffed toy.*

August 22

*What other toys did
you like to play with?*

August 23

*Did you have to abide
by a curfew as a youth?*

August 24

*Describe any "follow the
leader" games you pla yed.*

August 25

Phones have changed over the years. Describe how you used a phone to call up a childhood friend.

Did you ever have a fire in your home or accidentally catch something on fire?

*Tell about going to box
socials or pot lucks.*

*Tell about an incident
when you were very angry
with your mom or dad.*

Tell about an incident when your
mom or dad was very angry with you.

August 30

Share a memory
involving an outhouse.

August 31

Do you remember any Labor
Day traditions of your youth?

September 1

VJ Day...Do you have a memory involving the end of World War II?
If not, then share a memory of Vietnam.

Back-To-School-Days...
What do you remember about that big yearly "First Day of School"?

*Tell about your school
year calendar.*

September 4

Tell about a school bully.

September 5

What do you remember
doing at recess?

September 6

Tell about the playground
equipment at your grade school.

September 7

Did your parents ever make you
wear something stupid to school?

September 8

Tell about who you thought was
the smartest kid in school and why.

September 9

Tell about the naughtiest
kid in school.

September 10

How did you
experience the 9/11 attacks?

September 11

September 12

Name the schools
that you went to.

September 13

What was your most
embarrassing school moment?

September 14

Where did you usually buy
the clothes you wore?

September 15

*Describe a typical school
day outfit in grade school…*

In high school…

September 16

*If you were ever in
a fight, tell about it.*

September 17

*Name the grade school
teachers you remember.*

*Name the Jr. High
teachers you remember.*

*Name the High School
teachers you remember.*

*Tell about a teacher
who meant alot to
you and why.*

September 21

*If you ever had a hero,
tell who and why.*

September 22

*Were there any negative role
models who influenced you?*

September 23

*How did you get to
and from school?*

September 24

What were your school colors?

September 25

*What was your
school mascot?*

September 26

*Tell any sports you played
in Jr. High or High School.*

September 27

*What was your favorite sport
to participate in or watch?*

September 28

*What was the biggest physical
problem you had to deal with?*

September 29

*Do you remember
a school custodian?*

September 30

*What is the worst trick that
you remember a student
playing on a teacher?*

October 1

*What is the meanest thing
you ever saw a teacher do
to a student?*

October 2

Tell about school lunches.
Did you have a lunch box?
What did you eat?

October 3

Did you ever have
a crush on a teacher?

October 4

*Do you have any special memories
about raking and burning leaves,
or mowing the lawn?*

October 5

*If you ever played in
the leaves, tell about it.*

October 6

Do you have some
good advice for me?

October 7

October 8

Share some good advice
that <u>YOU</u> have recieved
in your lifetime.

October 9

October 10

Do you have any advice
on how to be wise with
my money?

October 11

*What allowance did you get at
different ages during your youth?*

October 12

*Did you have to do
anything to earn it?*

October 13

*Share a memory about
a bat in the house.*

October 14

*Relate a story about a
mouse in the house.*

October 15

*Tell about pulling
or losing a baby tooth.*

October 16

*Did you ever lose something
really important to you?*

October 17

Did you ever lose or break
something that belonged
to someone else?

October 18

Did you ever have a "good
friend" who did something
mean to you?

October 19

*Share a favorite
fall memory.*

October 20

Did you ever pick apples?

October 21

*What is the farthest you
ever ran or walked?*

October 22

*Did your High School
have cheerleaders?
What did they wear?*

*Can you recite any
of the school cheers?*

*How did your school
observe Homecoming?*

October 25

*Do you have any
special Homecoming
experiences to relate?*

October 26

*Tell about any other High School
extra-curricular activities.*

October 27

*Tell a story about a time when
you dressed up in a costume.*

October 28

Share a memory about
being very scared.

October 29

What did people
do at Halloween?

October 30

Do you have a special
Halloween memory?

October 31

Did you ever tell ghost stories?

November 1

Do you have a good ghost or
haunted house story to relate?

November 2

Tell about how you first
met my grandmother?

November 3

*What qualities first
attracted you to her?*

November 4

*Tell about your
wedding day.*

November 5

*What would you like me
to know about my mom?*

November 6

*What would you like me
to know about my dad?*

November 7

Tell me about the day I was born.

*Who was president
when you were born?*

When did you cast your first
Presidential vote and for whom?

_____

_____

_____

_____

_____

_____

November 10

Veteran's Day…
Name the veterans in your family
and times during which they served.

_____

_____

_____

_____

_____

_____

_____

November 11

*What was your most prized
possession as a child?*

November 12

*Do you have a story about standing
up against odds for something you
really believed in?*

November 13

*Did you ever feel a hatred for
another person? Explain.*

November 14

*Tell about the best birthday
present you ever received.*

November 15

*Was an injustice
ever done to you?*

November 16

*Did you ever make a purchase
you later regretted?*

November 17

*Tell about a memorable
birthday cake?*

November 18

*Have you ever had
a recurring dream?*

November 19

*Many people remember just
what they were doing when they
heard of the assassination of
John F. Kennedy. If you are not
old enough to have that time
etched in your memory, relate
any other childhood story.*

November 20

Did you ever chew tobacco?

November 21

Did you have a watch as a child? What was it like?

November 22

Share a memory about a weather-related school cancellation.

November 23

*Tell about Thanksgiving
traditions of your youth.*

November 24

*What foods were on your
Thanksgiving table?*

November 25

Share a favorite
Thanksgiving memory.

November 26

Do you have any ice
skating memories to share?

November 27

What hobbies or collections
did you have as a youth?

November 28

Tell about the day
my parent was born.

November 29

How did you choose the
name for that child?

November 30

*Please list your children's full
names and dates of birth.*

December 1

*On the next pages please share
some stories about my parent.*

December 2

December 5

December 6

Pearl Harbor Day…
If you are not old enough to relate
a memory of that day, relate any
other childhood remembrance.

December 7

Tell about something you built,
designed, or made as a youth.

December 8

Tell about your favorite stores to browse in as a child.

What did you like to look at there?

December 9

What did you first buy using your own money?

December 10

Were you ever in a church or school Christmas or Holiday pageant?

December 11

When did you put up your Christmas tree?
Where did you get them?

December 12

How did you decorate your trees?

December 13

Did you hang a Christmas stocking?

December 14

Did your Grandpa or Grandma ever make gifts for you? Tell about them.

December 15

Did your mom or dad ever make gifts for you? What?

December 16

*Tell about the best Christmas
present you ever received.*

_____

_____

_____

_____

_____

_____

_____

_____

_____

_____

_____

December 17

*Tell about something special
you gave to your mom.*

_____

_____

_____

_____

_____

_____

_____

_____

_____

December 18

Tell about something special
you gave to your dad.

December 19

Tell about the worst Christmas
present you ever received.

December 20

Tell about your experiences
with Santa Claus.

December 21

Did you ever go
Christmas caroling?

December 22

Did your family observe
the birth of Jesus at
Christmas? In what ways?

December 23

Tell about Holiday celebrations
at a relative's house.

December 24

*Do you remember
a "best" Christmas?*

December 25

*Share any other
Christmas memory.*

December 26

Is there anything else that you would like me to know about your childhood?

December 27

December 28

Do you remember celebrating any special wedding anniversaries of your parents or grandparents?

December 29

What special memories do you have of New Year's Eve or New Year's Day?

December 30

If you were to make a New Year's Resolution this year, what might it be?

December 31

Memory Journals
for Special People

Grandma, Tell Me Your Memories – Heirloom Edition

Grandpa, Tell Me Your Memories – Heirloom Edition

Mom, Share Your Life With Me – Heirloom Edition

Dad, Share Your Life With Me – Heirloom Edition

Grandma, Tell Me Your Memories

Grandpa, Tell Me Your Memories

Mom, Share Your Life With Me

Dad, Share Your Life With Me

To the Best of My Recollection

To My Dear Friend

My Days...My Pictures

My Days...My Writings

My Life...My Thoughts

Sisters

Mom, Tell Me One More Story...Your Story of Raising Me

Dad, Tell Me One More Story...Your Story of Raising Me